Usborne Spotter's Guides
DOGS

Harry Glover

Illustrated by John Francis
and Andy Martin

Edited by Alastair Smith, Rosamund Kidman Cox and Tim Dowley
Designed by Karen Tomlins and Joanne Kirkby
Digital illustrations by Verinder Bhachu
Cover designer: Michael Hill
Series designer: Laura Fearn
Consultant: Hazel Palmer

Acknowledgements: Cover © Jane Burton/Warren Photographic;
1 © Robert Dowling/Corbis; 2-3 © Jim Richardson/Corbis;
5 © Robert Dowling/Corbis; 6-7 © Yann Arthus-Bertrand/Corbis;
56 © Kevin R. Morris/Corbis; 58-59 © Joe McDonald/Corbis

This edition first published in 2006 by Usborne Publishing Ltd.,
Usborne House, 83-85 Saffron Hill, London, EC1N 8RT, England.
www.usborne.com

Printed in China

CONTENTS

HOW TO USE THIS BOOK

This book is an identification guide to dog breeds. Take it with you whenever you are likely to see dogs – whether you go out walking, to the park or to a dog show.

Originally, most dog breeds were developed to do a certain job. In this book the breeds are arranged into groups according to the jobs for which they were used.

Next to each picture is a short description of the breed. It tells you where the breed originated, its colouring, temperament and height.

There is a chart on pages 62-63. It lists all the breeds featured in this book. When you spot a certain breed, jot down the date that you saw it on the chart. You'll soon build a record of the breeds that you've spotted.

Name of breed	Date
Löwchen	08/06/06
Lurcher	28/06/06
Malinois	05/07/06
Maltese	10/01/07
Maremma	10/11/06

Fill in the chart like this.

When you spot a breed, make a tick in the circle next to its picture.

Throughout this book, you will find suggested links to dogs websites. For a complete list of links and instructions, turn to page 61.

DOG BREEDING

Dogs have been bred for thousands of years – originally to make types that were suited to particular purposes, such as hunting, pulling sledges or guarding. Today's dog breeds started in this way.

Today, dogs are bred more for their beauty than for their qualities as working dogs. However, many retain their ancestors' instincts. For example, a dog that was originally bred to hunt things will tend to chase other animals.

Originally, dalmatians were bred for stamina. Today, they are bred just for their looks, but they have the same boundless energy as their ancestors.

LOOKING AT DOGS

Dogs and their body parts are described
with particular words. The most important
ones are shown on this picture of a beagle.

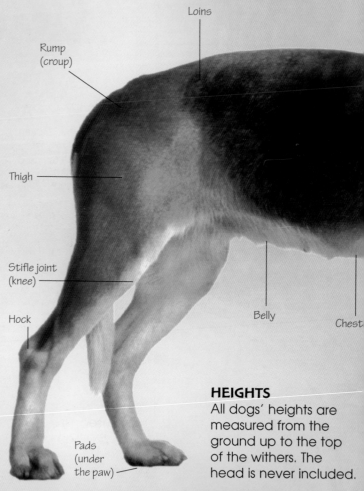

Loins

Rump
(croup)

Thigh

Stifle joint
(knee)

Hock

Belly

Chest

Pads
(under
the paw)

HEIGHTS

All dogs' heights are
measured from the
ground up to the top
of the withers. The
head is never included.

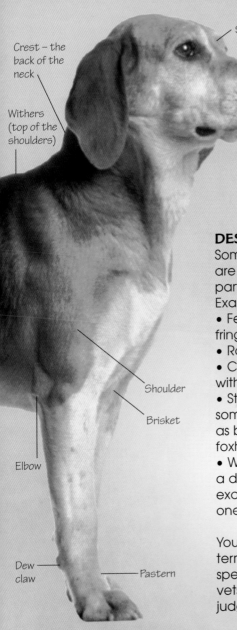

Crest – the back of the neck

Withers (top of the shoulders)

Stop – an indentation between the eyes, where the skull and nose meet.

Muzzle

Shoulder

Brisket

Elbow

Dew claw

Pastern

DESCRIBING DOGS

Some breeds' features are described in particular ways. Examples include:

- Feathering – long fringes of body hair.
- Racy – slightly built.
- Cobby – heavy, with a short back.
- Stern – the tail of some breeds, such as beagles and foxhounds.
- Wall eyes – eyes of a different colour, for example one blue, one white.

You may hear these terms used by specialists, such as vets, breeders, or judges at dog shows.

7

For a link to a design-a-dog game, turn to page 61.

MARKINGS

Occasionally, the names given to dogs' markings are unusual, and don't give much of a clue as to what the animal's coat really looks like. These pictures explain some of the more unusual names.

Black and tan

Blue

Brindle

Bronze

Buff

Chestnut

Grizzle

Harlequin

Liver

Merle and white

Mouse-grey

Pied

Roan

Salt and pepper

Tricolour

Wheaten

For a link to a website about different breeds of dogs, turn to page 61.

TAILS

When you are identifying breeds, look at the tails. Some breeds hold theirs in a distinctive way, as shown here.

Carried upright

Curled

Set high

Tails come in all shapes and sizes. You may see dogs with short tails that have been surgically removed. This is called docking. It is done when the puppy is very young. The argument in favour of docking is that long tails left on working dogs are often injured when the animal is working. Docking dogs' tails purely for fashion reasons is now illegal in some countries.

Set low

Long, flowing

EARS

Dogs' distinctive ears can help you to identify them. However, in some countries the natural shape of the ear is altered by removing part of it so that the remaining part sticks up. This operation is called cropping. In some countries it is illegal.

Erect

Semi-erect

Pendent (hanging)

9

PEDIGREE

If a dog has ancestors of the same breed, which have been recorded for at least three generations, it is classed as a pedigree dog. Pedigree dogs have been bred for centuries, especially in the Far East and Middle East. Today, they are bred all over the world.

Pedigree registration is controlled by organizations such as kennel clubs. Pedigree breeders usually register puppies soon after they are born. If you buy a pedigree puppy, make sure that you are given its pedigree history, written on an official certificate, when you take it home.

Family tree of a pedigree Dalmatian

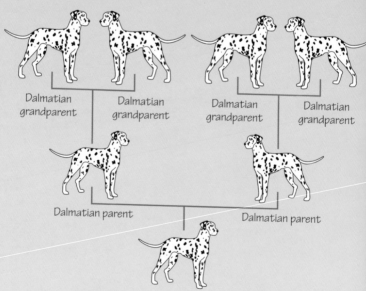

Dalmatian grandparent

Dalmatian grandparent

Dalmatian grandparent

Dalmatian grandparent

Dalmatian parent

Dalmatian parent

This dog can produce pedigree Dalmatians

CROSS-BRED DOGS

If a dog's parents are of different breeds then it is called a cross-bred dog. For example, if the father is a Golden Retriever and the mother is a German Shepherd, the dog is a Golden Retriever-German Shepherd cross.

Family tree of a cross-bred dog

Golden Retriever   German Shepherd

Cross-bred dog

MONGREL DOGS

A mongrel is a dog of mixed breed whose parents are either not known, or are themselves cross-bred or mongrel.

Family tree of a mongrel

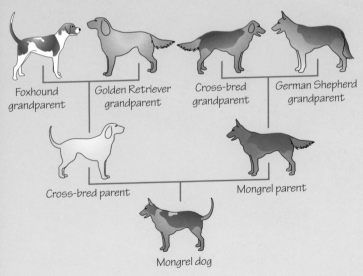

Foxhound grandparent   Golden Retriever grandparent   Cross-bred grandparent   German Shepherd grandparent

Cross-bred parent   Mongrel parent

Mongrel dog

TYPES OF DOG

GUARD DOGS
These dogs were originally bred to guard people and property. Some of them were used for hunting, too. They come from many parts of the world.

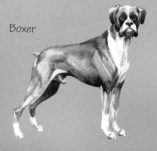

Boxer

HERDING DOGS
These dogs were bred to herd other animals – usually sheep or cattle. They were also used as guard dogs. Many are still used for herding in their places of origin.

Border Collie

GUN DOGS
Gun dogs were bred to help hunters. Some are used to find and chase out animals for hunters to shoot. Others are taught to fetch shot animals, usually birds.

Cocker Spaniel

HEELING DOGS
These little dogs were bred to drive cattle. If the cattle stop, the dogs nip their heels, then back off before the animal can kick. This is how they get their name.

Pembroke Corgi

For a link to a quiz about working dogs, turn to page 61.

RUNNING DOGS

Running dogs were bred to chase game. Different types have been bred all over the world, but they all share certain traits: they all have long legs, they are lightly built and they can run very fast.

Whippet

HAULING DOGS

These dogs were specially bred to pull sledges over snow and ice in the Arctic. Many are now popular pets. Some are still used to pull sledges for sport and fun.

Alaskan Malamute

SCENT HUNTERS

These dogs have a good sense of smell, which they use to hunt prey. In their home countries they are popular for hunting.

Wire-haired Dachshund

COMPANION DOGS

Dogs of this type were originally bred for a variety of uses. Their small size and friendliness made them popular as pets.

Pekingese

HUNTING TERRIERS

Hunting terriers were bred to chase animals such as foxes, badgers and rats.

Dandie Dinmont Terrier

13

GUARD DOGS

➡ KEESHOND
From Netherlands. Originally
used to guard barges, so
also called Dutch Barge
Dog. Good companion.
Fox-like head, and
neck ruff. Long
coat. Grey, with
cream legs and
feet. 40-48cm.

"Spectacle"
markings
around
eyes

Feathering
on thighs

⬅ SCHIPPERKE
From Belgium. Also
called Belgian Barge
Dog. Loyal. Short,
smooth coat, longer
on neck. Usually
black. 30-33cm.

➡ BULLDOG
British breed. Brave
and determined. Once
used for bull baiting. Big
head for body. Friendly.
Good watchdog. Short
coat. Any colour, except
black. 31-36cm.

Legs
wide apart

14

For a link to a site where you can meet virtual dogs, turn to page 61.

➡ BOXER

German breed.
Very strong and active.
Good guard, but fine
house pet, too. Short,
smooth coat. Can
be red, fawn or
brindle, often with
white markings.
53-60cm.

Big square
head with
prominent stop

The stop is
very prominent

Docked
tail

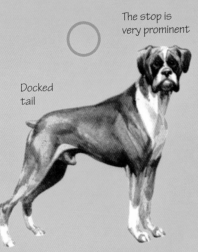

⬅ BULLMASTIFF

British, bred from
Bulldog and Mastiff.
Lively, loyal and
fearless. Short coat.
Red, fawn or brindle.
61-68cm.

➡ ROTTWEILER

German. Used by
police and armed
forces. Intelligent
but strong willed.
Short coat. Black
and tan. 56-68cm.

GUARD DOGS

➡ GREAT DANE
First used in Germany,
France and Denmark,
to hunt wild boar.
Large but friendly. Will
guard. Short, smooth
coat. Fawn, black,
blue, brindle, or
harlequin. 73-81cm.

Drooping, pendent
ears are cropped
in North America

Tail
held
low

Docked tail

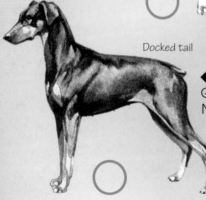

⬅ DOBERMANN
German. Brave and loyal.
Needs training. Short
coat. Black, brown
or blue with tan
markings. 66-68cm.

Ideally, the spots
should not overlap

➡ DALMATIAN
Thought to be
from Dalmatia,
Croatia. Lively and
friendly. Needs lots of
exercise. Short, sleek
coat. White, with black
or liver spots. 55-60cm.

➡ ANATOLIAN KARABASH

From Turkey, where it was first used to guard sheep. Good guard, but needs training. Short coat. Cream, fawn, brindle or black. 66-76cm.

⬅ LEONBERGER

Rare German breed. Friendly house dog and brave guard. Long, softish coat. Golden to red. 68-78cm.

➡ ESTRELA MOUNTAIN DOG

From Estrela mountains, Portugal. Rare. Strong, intelligent and active. Usually fawn, black mask. 63-71cm.

17

GUARD DOGS

➡ NEWFOUNDLAND
From Newfoundland,
Canada. Good
swimmer. Very strong,
but gentle and friendly.
Long coat. Black or
bronze.
66-71cm.

Pendent ears

Thick coat
protects
against bad
weather

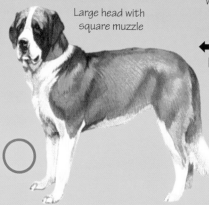

Large head with
square muzzle

⬅ ST BERNARD
Bred by St Bernard
Hospice, Switzerland,
to rescue travellers
lost in snow. Heavy,
strong but gentle.
Rough or smooth
coat. Usually red
and white.
66-71cm.

➡ BERNESE MOUNTAIN DOG
From Switzerland. Was
used to pull carts. Easy
to train. Long, soft coat.
Black, brown or tan
markings, white
chest. 61-66cm.

➡ GIANT SCHNAUZER

From Bavaria, Germany, where it was used to herd cattle. Energetic. Good guard dog, but needs training. Wiry coat. Black or salt and pepper. 71cm.

The ears are normally pendent, but this dog's are cropped

Beard and whiskers

Pendent ears

Bushy eyebrows

Docked tail

Beard and whiskers

⬅ STANDARD SCHNAUZER

From Bavaria, Germany. Once used to kill rats and other pests. Lively, keen watch dog. Needs training. Wiry coat. Black or salt and pepper. 45-51cm.

This dog's ears have been cropped

Docked tail

Beard and whiskers

➡ MINIATURE SCHNAUZER

From Bavaria, Germany. Loyal, active and alert. Rough, hard coat. Black or salt and pepper. 30-45cm.

19

GUN DOGS

➡ WELSH SPRINGER SPANIEL
Originally from Wales.
Smaller than English
Springer. Used for fetching
shot birds from water.
Lively, energetic pet.
Straight, thick, silky coat.
Red and white. 45-48cm.

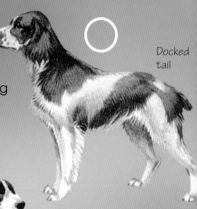

Docked
tail

⬅ ENGLISH SPRINGER SPANIEL
Old spaniel breed. Finds,
drives out and retrieves
game. Active. Needs
regular exercise. Usually
liver and white, or black
and white. 51cm.

Top-knot of
curly hair

Short,
smooth
tail tip

➡ IRISH WATER SPANIEL
Old breed. Good at
retrieving game from
water. Playful and
active. Stiff, short curly
coat. Dark liver colour.
51-58cm.

➡ COCKER SPANIEL

British. Very popular show dog and pet. Intelligent, but needs lots of exercise. Longish coat. Many colours, such as black, red, liver or golden. 38-49cm.

Long, drooping, pendent ears

Stop

Long, drooping, pendent ears

⬅ AMERICAN COCKER SPANIEL

Smaller than English Cocker. Lively. Coat feathered on body and legs. Thick coat needs regular grooming. Buff, black, or mixed colours. 34-39cm.

Long, drooping, pendent ears

➡ FIELD SPANIEL

British. Friendly. Shorter legs, longer body than other Spaniels. Medium length coat. Most often black, red, liver or roan. 45cm.

GUN DOGS

➡ SUSSEX SPANIEL
From England. Rare.
Active, friendly and
very easy to train.
Heavy body, with
short legs. Always
liver, with gold tips.
38-40cm.

Docked tail

Docked
tail

Long,
heavy body

⬅ CLUMBER SPANIEL
From Clumber Park,
England. Strong and
friendly. Heavy, with
short legs. Close, silky
coat. White with lemon
markings. 48-51cm.

Short legs

Long, wavy
coat

Long tail

**➡ SMALL
MÜNSTERLANDER**
From Westphalia,
Germany. Used for
finding and retrieving
game. Friendly. White
and brown, with roan
marks. 48-56cm.

Deep
chest

➡ CHESAPEAKE BAY RETRIEVER

Originally from east coast of USA. Intelligent, but strong willed and needs training. Dark brown to faded tan. 53-66cm.

Short, slightly wavy coat

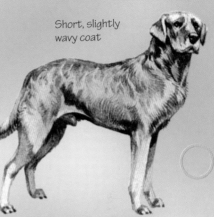

⬅ LABRADOR RETRIEVER

From Newfoundland, Canada, and named after Labrador, a region there. Popular gun dog, guide dog, police dog and pet. Black, chocolate or golden. 54-57cm.

Short, thick coat

➡ CURLY-COATED RETRIEVER

British working dog. Strong gun dog. Can retrieve from water. Active, intelligent. Black or liver colour. 63-68cm.

Tightly curled coat

GUN DOGS

➤ FLAT-COATED RETRIEVER

British. Good retrieving dog.
Strong and intelligent. Playful
pet. Black or liver colour.
51-61cm.

Flat, springy
coat

Feathering
on tail and thighs

Feathering
on front legs

Flat or wavy coat
with feathering

◄ GOLDEN RETRIEVER

Popular British breed.
Works well. Good house
dog, but needs lots of
exercise. Any shade
of cream or gold.
51-61cm.

Docked tail

➤ WEIMARANER

From Weimar,
Germany. Friendly,
alert and active.
Smooth coat. Silvery
mouse-grey colour.
56-63cm.

Very short,
fine coat

➤ ENGLISH SETTER
Old British breed. Good family pet. Black and white, lemon and white, liver and white, or tricolour. 61-68cm.

Stop

Feathering on legs and tail

Long, silky, slightly wavy coat

◄ GORDON SETTER
Originally from Scotland. Heavy breed. Loyal, but tricky to train. Long, soft and glossy coat. Shiny black with tan markings. 66cm.

Stop

➤ IRISH SETTER
From Ireland. Works well when trained. Very lively. Long neck and head. Long, silky coat. Always chestnut. 61cm.

Deep chest

25

GUN DOGS

➡ VIZSLA
From Hungary. Finds
and retrieves shot
game birds. Gentle and
affectionate, though
very active. Short coat.
Sandy yellow.
57-64cm.

Long, drooping,
pendent ears

Short, glossy coat

⬅ POINTER
Originally from Spain.
Points at game bird with
nose, body and tail in
straight line. Very
active. Black, or
another colour with
white. 61-68cm.

Docked tail

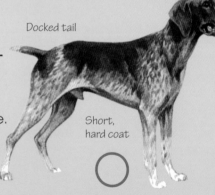
Short,
hard coat

**➡ GERMAN SHORT-
HAIRED POINTER**
Finds and retrieves
game. Friendly, but
needs lots of exercise.
Good guard. Liver,
or liver and white
spotted or flecked.
63-66cm.

➡ DRENTSE PATRIJSHOND
From Netherlands. Good at hunting partridge. Will fetch game from water. Thick, longish coat. White, with brown or orange. 56-63cm.

Feathered ears

Long, feathered tail

Fairly smooth coat

⬅ BRITTANY SPANIEL
Originally from Brittany, France. Fast, intelligent. Good pet. White, with brown or orange. 45-51cm.

Ears hang flat

➡ LARGE MÜNSTERLANDER
From Germany. Good gun dog and pest catcher. Active. Needs training. White with black patches. 58-63cm.

Long, slightly wavy coat

HERDING DOGS

➡ MAREMMA
From Central Italy.
Good herder and
guard. Intelligent,
though independent.
Black nose. Usually
white, can have
lemon or fawn
markings. 61-74cm.

Longish coat

Long
neck hair

Long
neck
hair

Short,
wavy body
hair

⬅ KUVASZ
From Hungary. Used
for guarding sheep
and cattle. Loyal and
protective. Always
white. 67-76cm.

Thick coat

⬅ PYRENEAN
MOUNTAIN DOG
From Pyrenees
mountains on the
French-Spanish border.
Guards sheep. Large
and strong, though
gentle. All white, or
white with markings.
66-81cm.

➡ GROENENDAEL

Sheepdog from Belgium.
Intelligent and obedient.
Very good watchdog.
Fairly long coat. Black.
58-62cm.

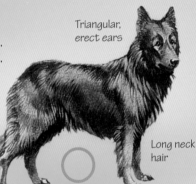

Triangular,
erect ears

Long neck
hair

Triangular,
erect ears

⬅ MALINOIS

Belgian Shepherd Dog.
Smooth coat, similar to
German Shepherd Dog.
Fawn or red colouring,
with black hair tips.
58-62cm.

➡ TERVUEREN

From Belgium. Looks like
Groenendael, but is
reddish-fawn with black
hair tips and tail tip.
58-62cm.

HERDING DOGS

➡ GERMAN SHEPHERD DOG
Used by police, armed
forces and as guide dog
for blind. Intelligent,
loyal and easy to
train. Any colour.
56-66cm.

Triangular,
erect ears

Tail hangs in
slight curve

Smooth
coat

Long outer
coat

Full neck
ruff

Semi-erect
ears

⬅ ROUGH COLLIE
Originally from Scotland,
where it was used to herd
sheep. Friendly and active.
Needs regular grooming.
Usually sable and white, blue
and white or tricolour. 61-68cm.

Semi-erect
ears

➡ SMOOTH COLLIE
British. Less common
than Rough Collie.
Has a short,
smooth, hard
coat. 51-61cm.

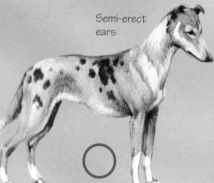

➡ OLD ENGLISH SHEEPDOG

Often called "bobtail". Good guard dog. Strong and active. Needs daily grooming. Grey, blue or grizzle, with or without white. Over 56cm.

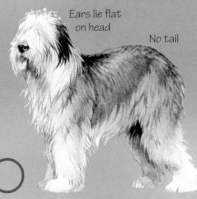

Ears lie flat on head

No tail

Beard on both sides of muzzle

⬅ BEARDED COLLIE

Originally from Scotland. Used mainly as sheepdog. Loyal, loving pet. Long coat. Can be blue, grey-black, red and white. 51-56cm.

Semi-erect ears

Full neck ruff

➡ SHETLAND SHEEPDOG

Originally from Shetland Islands, Scotland. Looks like small Rough Collie. Ideal family pet. Colours include black and white, black and tan, merle, sable. 35-37cm.

31

HERDING DOGS

➡ TIBETAN TERRIER
From mountains of Tibet. Once used to herd sheep, goats and cattle. Lively, active and intelligent. Long, fine double coat. White, cream, grey, golden and black. 35-40cm.

Tail curled over back

Large, round feet

Tail curled over back

Corded coat

⬅ PULI
From Hungary. Woolly undercoat. Long outer coat hangs in cords and needs regular attention. Can work in cold conditions. White, grey or black. 38-44cm.

➡ KOMONDOR
From Hungary. Thick coat hangs in long cords. Bold, hard worker. Loyal, protective companion. Always white. 56-81cm.

Curved tail

Corded coat

Hair falls over eyes

➡ BORDER COLLIE
Good working sheepdog, from northern England. Very intelligent and energetic. Needs regular, hard exercise. Longish, smooth or slightly wavy coat. Usually black and white. 51-53cm.

Eyebrows hang over eyes

⬇ BRIARD
French breed. Intelligent and active. Square look to body. Can be any colour apart from white. 56-58cm.

Feathered, curved tail

Docked tail

➡ BOUVIER DES FLANDRES
Bred in Flanders, Belgium, to herd cattle. Active. Rough, wiry coat. Has eyebrows, beard and moustache. Drab yellow, grey or black. 59-68cm.

HEELING DOGS

➡ KELPIE
Australian. Bred from
sheepdogs. Hard working.
Tough and active. Short
coat. Black, red
or chocolate.
43-51cm.

*Erect
ears*

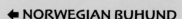

*Tail curled
over back and
to one side*

⬅ NORWEGIAN BUHUND
Farm dog. Brave and
intelligent. Long, thick coat,
which is longest on body
and neck. Fawn, red
or yellowish. 45cm.

*Speckled
coat*

**➡ AUSTRALIAN
CATTLE DOG**
Bred from Smooth Collie,
dingo (wild dog) and
Dalmatian. Tough. Used for
driving cattle. Short coat.
Red or blue speckled.
45-51cm.

➡ VALLHUND

From Sweden.
Also called
"Västgötaspets".
Almost died out in
1940s. Has short coat.
Can be grey, brownish
or red. 38-49cm.

Very short
tail

Erect ears

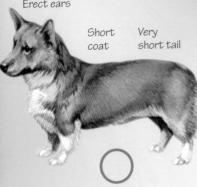

Short
coat

Very
short tail

⬅ PEMBROKE CORGI

Originally used to drive
cattle and ponies in
South Wales. Now a
popular pet. Will nip.
Can be red, black,
fawn, black or tan.
Can have white
markings. 25-30cm.

Large, erect
ears point out

➡ CARDIGAN CORGI

Another driving dog
from South Wales.
Longer body and
larger ears than
Pembroke. Short
coat. Will nip. Any
colour except
all-white. 30cm.

Tail looks like
fox's brush

RUNNING DOGS

➡ SALUKI
Bred in Middle East to hunt deer
and antelope. Loyal and active.
Long ears. White, golden, black
and tan. 58-71cm.

Smooth coat

Feathered,
curved tail

Feathered
legs

⬅ SLOUGHI
Bred in North Africa to hunt small
game. Rare. Looks like smooth
Saluki. Active. Usually sandy, can
be brindle. 56-76cm.

➡ BORZOI
Bred in Russia to hunt
game and wolves.
Active and friendly.
Various colours.
69-79cm.

Feathered
tail

Long, silky
coat

Long tail,
curved
at tip

⬅ AFGHAN HOUND
Bred in Afghanistan to
hunt deer. Long, silky
coat, feathered ears.
All colours. 64-74cm.

➡ IRISH WOLFHOUND
Irish breed. One of largest breeds. Good natured. Rough, hard coat. Grey, brindle, red, fawn, black or pure white. Over 71cm.

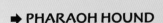

⬅ DEERHOUND
Scottish breed. Smaller and lighter than Irish Wolfhound. Once used to hunt deer. Thick, rough coat. Grey, yellowish or brindle. 71-76cm.

➡ PHARAOH HOUND
Ancient breed. Probably North African. Smooth coat. Often rich red, with white on chest. 53-63cm.

Large, erect ears

⬅ IBIZAN HOUND
From island of Ibiza, Spain. Used as hunter and watchdog. Rough or smooth coat. 61-66cm.

RUNNING DOGS

➡ GREYHOUND
Ancient breed, used for hunting hares and rabbits. Very fast. Will chase small animals. Now used for track racing. Smooth coat. Most colours. 71-76cm.

Long, low-set tail

Deep chest

⬅ LURCHER
Gypsies' traditional hunting dog. Usually greyhound-collie cross. Rough coated. Fawn, grey or black. 71-76cm.

➡ WHIPPET
Originally from northern England. Bred for racing. Looks like miniature greyhound. Friendly. Smooth coat. Any colour or colour mix. 44-51cm.

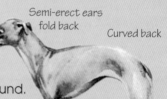

Semi-erect ears fold back

Curved back

Semi-erect ears folded back

Arched back

⬅ ITALIAN GREYHOUND
Originally from Italy. Smallest running dog. Quiet and friendly. Smooth coat. Fawn, black, cream, white, pied. 32-35cm.

HAULING DOGS

➡ ALASKAN MALAMUTE
From northern Canada. Large, strong dog. Loves people, but can be aggressive to other dogs. Grey to black, white under body. 58-71cm.

Mask-like markings on head

Thick coat

Tail curves over back

⬅ SIBERIAN HUSKY
From Siberia, northern Russia. Used for herding, sledge pulling. Good worker. Friendly pet. Long, thick, soft coat. All colours, with white markings. 51-59cm.

Small, erect ears

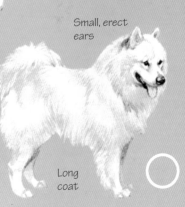

Tail curves over back

➡ SAMOYED
Russian breed. Still used in sledge races. Can round up reindeer. Good pet. Silver-white. May have cream marks. 45-53cm.

Long coat

SCENT HUNTERS

➡ FINNISH SPITZ
Originally from Finland,
where it was used for
hunting. Good guard.
Noisy. Longish coat.
Red-gold to red-brown.
39-44cm.

*Erect,
pointed ears*

*Tightly-
curled tail*

⬅ ELKHOUND
Originally from Norway,
where it was used to hunt
elk. Can stand cold weather.
Independent, energetic.
Thick, hard coat. Grey.
47-52cm.

*Ridge of hairs
on back*

➡ RHODESIAN
RIDGEBACK
From Rhodesia (now
Zimbabwe), Africa.
Used for guarding and
hunting. Strong fighter.
Short, glossy coat.
Yellowish to reddish.
61-68cm.

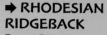

For a link to a site about the history of the dog family, turn to page 61.

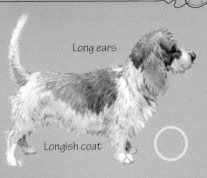

Long ears

Longish coat

➡ BASSET GRIFFON VENDÉEN
From southwest France, where it was used for hunting hares. Active. Mostly white, with markings. 34-43cm.

Tail carried high

⬅ BEAGLE
English breed. Originally used for hunting. Active. Very friendly pet. Short, hard coat. Various colours. 34-40cm.

Very long, pendent ears

➡ BASSET HOUND
French breed. Good natured. Lively. Smooth, short coat. Various colours. 33-38cm.

➡ BASENJI
From central Africa. Originally used to hunt antelope. Very friendly. Black, red, chestnut and white, or black and tan with white. 40-43cm.

Tail tightly curled

SCENT HUNTERS

➡ BLOODHOUND
Ancient breed, from
Normandy, northern
France. Great sense
of smell. Used to hunt
deer and track scent
of escaped prisoners.
Short, glossy coat.
Black or liver and
tan, sometimes red.
61-66cm.

Very long,
pendent ears

Loose
skin on
head

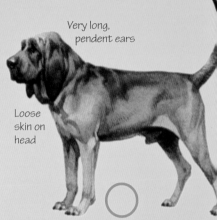

Long tail

⬅ FOXHOUND
Used in packs for hunting.
Friendly. Short, smooth coat.
Usually tan, with black and
white markings, or white with
black, tan or lemon marks.
53-63cm.

➡ OTTERHOUND
British breed, originally
to hunt otters. Swims
well. Longish, hard coat.
Usually fawn or grey with
black and tan markings.
61-66cm.

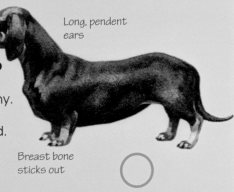

Long, pendent
ears

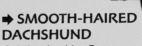

➡ SMOOTH-HAIRED
DACHSHUND
Originated in Germany.
Once used to pursue
badgers underground.
Also used to hunt in
packs. Short, smooth
coat. Any colour but
white. 13-23cm.

Breast bone
sticks out

⬇ LONG-HAIRED DACHSHUND
Bred for sport, but also very popular as
pet. Silky, longish coat. Brown, red, black
and tan or dapple colour. 13-23cm.

Feathered
body and tail

⬇ WIRE-HAIRED DACHSHUND
Has been used to hunt wild boar and
follow other game underground. Short
coat. All colours. 13-23cm.

Eyebrows

Feathered
body and
tail

Beard

43

COMPANION DOGS

➡ CHOW CHOW
Originally bred in China.
Popular pet. Looks a little
like a lion. Alert and
independent. Black, red,
blue, fawn or cream in
colour. 46-56cm.

Very thick coat

Tail curls
over hip

⬅ PUG
From China. Was popular
with English royal family in
1800s. Very loving pet. Short,
glossy coat. Fawn
or black. 33cm.

➡ LÖWCHEN
Probably comes from the
Mediterranean. Also called
"Little Lion Dog". Ancient,
rare breed. Long coat.
Friendly. Usually black, white,
grey or cream. 25cm.

Tufted
tail

Clipped
coat

Crest
of hair

⬅ CHINESE CRESTED DOG
Despite its name, probably
from Mexico or Africa, not China.
Almost hairless. Patches of pink,
blue, mauve or white. 33cm.

For a link to a website with a puppy slide show, turn to page 61.

➡ KING CHARLES SPANIEL

Favourite at court of King
Charles II of England. Gentle
and loving. Long, silky coat.
Black and tan, rich
red or tricolour. 25-27cm.

Short
muzzle

Long,
feathered
ears

⬅ CAVALIER KING CHARLES SPANIEL

Long, silky coat. Larger
than King Charles Spaniel.
Friendly. Black and tan, red
and white, red or tricolour.
31-33cm.

➡ TIBETAN SPANIEL

First bred by monks
of Tibet. Looks like
a Pekingese. Long,
smooth coat. Golden,
cream, white, black,
or tricolour. 24-28cm.

Curled tail

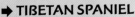

⬅ BICHON FRISE

Probably from Spain.
Friendly. Silky white coat,
often with grey patches
on skin. 20-30cm.

COMPANION DOGS

➡ JAPANESE CHIN
Probably originated in China, but became the pet of many Japanese emperors. Long coat. White with red or black patches. 30cm.

Rounded skull

⬅ PAPILLON
First bred in France. Called "Butterfly Dog" because of shape of its head and ears. Long coat. White with all colours except liver. 28cm.

➡ POMERANIAN
From Pomerania, Germany/Poland. Small version of Finnish Spitz. Red, blue, orange, white, black or brown. 28cm.

Tail lies flat over back

⬅ AFFENPINSCHER
Tiny dog, from Germany. Often shown in old Dutch paintings. Looks a little like a monkey. Wiry coat, usually black. Up to 28cm.

➡ SHIH TZU
Originally from China. Tiny but brave. Rounded skull, square muzzle. Playful. Long, straight coat. All colours. Up to 27cm.

Beard and whiskers

Tail curls over back

⬅ MALTESE
Very old breed, from Malta. Often painted in pictures as lap dog. Loyal. Short body and legs. Long, pure white coat. 20-25cm.

➡ PEKINGESE
Originally from China, where it was once a court pet. Long coat. Stubborn. All colours except liver. 15-25cm.

Tail curled over back

⬅ LHASA APSO
Originally from Tibet. Lively and assertive. Long, hard coat. Usually golden, sandy or grey. 25-28cm.

47

COMPANION DOGS

➡ AUSTRALIAN SILKY TERRIER
Bred in Australia from Yorkshire and Australian Terriers. Long, silky coat. Silver, or blue with tan marks. 22cm.

Small, erect ears

Very long coat with parting in middle

⬅ YORKSHIRE TERRIER
Tiny English Terrier. Very popular pet. Good rat and mouse catcher. Long, straight, silky coat. Should be dark blue and tan coloured. 18-20cm.

➡ GRIFFON BRUXELLOIS
Originally from Belgium. Lively little dog. Rough, wiry, short coat. Red, black or black and tan. 18-20cm.

Docked tail

Heavy whiskers

➡ GRIFFON BRABANÇON
From Belgium. Similar to Griffon Bruxellois, but smooth-coated. Also called "Smooth Griffon". 18-20cm.

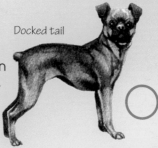

Docked tail

➡ CHIHUAHUA, SMOOTH-COAT

Mexican. Smallest breed. Also called "Ornament Dog" or "Pillow Dog". Bold. Can be aggressive. Fine coat. 15-23cm.

Flattish tail

⬅ CHIHUAHUA, LONG-COAT

Silky coat with feathering. Same stature and character as smooth-coated version. Can be any colour. 15-23cm.

➡ POODLES

Probably originated in Germany. Easy to train. Coat curly, hard and thick. Any colour. Split into categories: "Toy", "Miniature" and "Standard". Category sizes vary according to different rules of various kennel clubs around the world.

Standard

Coats have been trimmed into "lion cut"

Toy

Miniature

COMPANION DOGS

➡ FRENCH BULLDOG
Has large ears, which look
like a bat's. Very friendly
little dog. Short coat.
Brindle, fawn or pied.
26-35cm.

Docked
tail

White
collar

⬅ BOSTON TERRIER
Originally from the USA.
Lively and clever. Short,
glossy coat. Broad, round
head. Brindle and white,
or black and white. 40cm.

➡ ENGLISH TOY TERRIER
Also called "Black and
Tan". Miniature version
of Manchester Terrier.
Brave and alert. Good rat
hunter. Smooth, short coat.
Black and tan. 25-30cm.

Docked
tail

⬅ MINIATURE PINSCHER
German breed. Lively and
spirited, but easily trained.
Short, smooth coat. Red,
black, blue or chocolate
with tan markings. 25-30cm.

HUNTING TERRIERS

➡ MANCHESTER TERRIER
Originally from Manchester, northern England, where it was used to catch rats. Intelligent and lively. Short, glossy coat. Black and tan. 38-40cm.

Short, glossy coat

Egg-shaped head

⬅ BULL TERRIER
English breed. Friendly to people, but fights dogs. Short, smooth coat. White, sometimes with markings, or coloured. 35-40cm.

Semi-erect ears

➡ STAFFORDSHIRE BULL TERRIER
From Staffordshire, England. Short, glossy coat. Very friendly with people, but loves to fight other dogs. Red, fawn, blue or black. 36-41cm.

Short legs

⬅ JACK RUSSELL TERRIER
British. Bred from several different types of terrier. Excellent pest catcher. Short or rough coated. White with coloured patches. 23-38cm.

51

HUNTING TERRIERS

➡ WEST HIGHLAND TERRIER
Originally from Scotland. Popular house pet. Good guard. Long, coarse coat, soft undercoat. Always white. Up to 28cm.

Small, upright tail

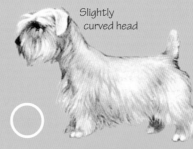

⬅ SCOTTISH TERRIER
Once called "Aberdeen Terrier". Show dog and pet. Intelligent. Wiry, longish coat. Black, flecked grey or brown. 25-28cm.

➡ SEALYHAM TERRIER
Originally from Wales, where it was used for hunting in packs. Long, wiry coat. White, sometimes with yellow markings on head and ears. 30cm.

Slightly curved head

➡ CAIRN TERRIER
Originally from Scotland. Similar to West Highland. Longish, hardish coat. Red, sandy, grey, mottled brown or off-black. 24-26cm.

Small, pointed, erect ears

➡ NORWICH TERRIER and NORFOLK TERRIER

British breeds, very similar to one another. Norwich has erect ears, Norfolk has semi-erect ears. Wiry coat. Red, black and tan, sandy or greyish colour. 25cm.

Erect ears

Docked tail

⬅ BORDER TERRIER

Very active breed. Rough, weatherproof coat. Red, wheaten, grey and tan or blue and tan colour. 26-30cm.

➡ DANDIE DINMONT TERRIER

Named after character in a book by Sir Walter Scott. Coat of mixed soft and hard hairs. Pepper or mustard colour. 20-28cm.

Large, wide head

Docked tail

⬅ AUSTRALIAN TERRIER

Popular in Australia and New Zealand. Strong and friendly. Hard, straight coat. Red, or blue and tan in colour. 25cm.

HUNTING TERRIERS

➡ AIREDALE TERRIER
Named after Aire Valley,
Yorkshire, England. Largest
terrier. Bred to hunt pests.
Strong but easy to train.
Rough, wiry coat. Black
or grey and tan. 55-61cm.

⬅ LAKELAND TERRIER
From northern England.
Used for hunting. Friendly.
Rough, thick coat. Various
colours. 37cm.

➡ WELSH TERRIER
Used in Wales to hunt.
Strong. Good guard dog
and house dog. Hard, wiry
coat. Black and tan. 39cm.

Semi-erect
ears carried
forward

Beard and
whiskers

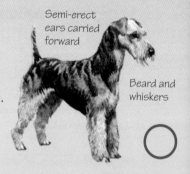

Beard
and
whiskers

⬅ KERRY BLUE TERRIER
Irish. Bred to hunt fox, badger
and otter. Popular show dog.
Friendly, but fights. Soft wavy
coat. Any blue shade.
46-48cm.

➡ IRISH TERRIER

From Ireland. Likes to fight, but friendly to people. Fairly short coat. Any shade of red. 45cm.

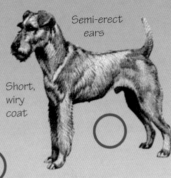

Semi-erect ears

Short, wiry coat

Top knot

Arched back

⬅ BEDLINGTON TERRIER

From northern England. Looks a little like a lamb. Brave and friendly. Good pet. Thick, wavy coat. Blue, liver, sandy or mixed colours. 40cm.

➡ FOX TERRIER, SMOOTH-COAT

From England. Lively and intelligent. Short, hard, smooth coat. Mainly white. 37-39cm.

Short back

Tapering head

Short back

Long, square muzzle

⬅ FOX TERRIER, WIRE-COAT

Similar to Smooth-coat, but with longer, wiry hair. White, some black or tan markings. 37-39cm.

CHOOSING A DOG

Dogs can be fantastic companions, and great fun. However, they need a lot of looking after. Make sure that you will be able to commit lots of time and energy to looking after your dog.

Find out as much as you can about the different breeds. Choose a dog that is the right size and temperament to suit your lifestyle.

PUPPIES

Choose a puppy that is friendly to you. However, beware of any that are too bold – they may be hard to train. Similarly, watch out for very shy ones. They may stay nervous all their lives.

If you want to buy a puppy, look for signs that it is healthy. The picture below shows some of the things to look for.

Check that the coat is healthy. A poor coat can be a sign of hard-to-treat skin problems.

Inspect the ears. Dirty ears are a clue that the pup may be ill.

Bright eyes are a sign of good general health.

Look for a full set of teeth. Bad teeth may signal illness.

DOG CARE

Grooming keeps your dog's skin healthy, and helps to get rid of any shed hairs. Get your puppy used to being groomed as soon as possible, so that the job is easy and stress-free for both of you.

Dogs over six months old should be bathed every few months, unless they are very dirty. Use a dog shampoo, and dry the dog with a towel reserved just for its own use. Drying will prevent your pet from catching a chill.

EQUIPMENT

• A metal comb, for long-haired dogs. Start grooming with this, to remove tangles and dirt.

• A hound glove. For smooth-coated dogs. The bristle side is for brushing, the velvet side for finishing off.

• A bristle brush, for long-haired dogs. Use this after you have finished with the metal comb.

• Coat clippers. These are for dogs that need special clipping, such as poodles or schnauzers.

• A two-sided brush. The metal bristles are to clean and untangle hair. The nylon bristles are for finishing off.

• Nail clippers. Only use these if you have been shown how.

57

For links to sites about choosing and looking after a dog, turn to page 61.

TRAINING – THE BASICS

The ancestors of domestic dogs lived in packs with a leader dog. Your dog will see you as its leader and will expect to obey you. Training is therefore very important. If it is done with patience and care the dog will enjoy being trained. You should start from the day your dog comes to live with you.

Remember that a dog can't understand what you are saying but it can interpret and remember sounds and tones of voice.

Never bully your dog by shouting at it or hitting it. If you catch it in the act of behaving badly tell it off in a stern voice. But if it behaves well, reward it with warm praise. Your dog will respond to you by remembering to do the things for which it is praised.

Best of all, if you want to train your dog thoroughly, seek out a dog training class – with a trainer that only uses non-violent methods.

A well-trained dog will obey you all the time – even when it is playing.

BODY LANGUAGE

A dog shows how it feels by the position of its body.
Here are some common body postures.

Alert and confident. The body is
held firm, with head up. The tail
is probably wagging.

Apologetic. If a dog is frightened
of you it will probably adopt
this position.

Playful. Crouching, ears up, tail
wagging. This happy dog wants
to play.

Afraid. The tail falls between the
legs, the body is held low and the
head is level with the back.

Wanting. A dog may do this when
it would like something from you,
such as affection or food.

Submissive. This frightened dog
has given in completely. There is no
greater sign of submission than this.

For a link to a website about dog-training, turn to page 61.

DOG OWNER'S CODE

- Train your dog. For best results, take your pet to obedience classes.
- Don't frighten, bully or hit your dog.
- Keep a collar with an identity tag on your dog.
- Control your dog at all times.
- Keep your dog on a lead near roads or farms.
- Regular exercise is vital.
- When exercising your dog, always take a poop scoop.
- Always dispose of your dog's mess properly.
- Give your dog its own bed.
- Feed your dog at the same time every day.
- Feed your dog from its own bowl.
- Keep your dog clean.
- Don't let your dog disturb other people.
- Don't let your dog wander off on its own.
- Register your dog with a vet.

USEFUL WORDS

Beard – thick hair on muzzle and chin.

Bat ears – broad, upright ears with round tips.

Bitch – female dog.

Blaze – white marking up face and between eyes.

Coursing – chasing game animals (usually hares) for sport.

Cropped ears – ears with hanging part removed.

Docked tail – tail that has had end removed.

Feathering – long fringe of hair.

Game – animals hunted for sport, such as birds, hares and rabbits.

Mask – dark colour on muzzle.

Muzzle – snout, including mouth and nose.

Pests – animals considered destructive and harmful.

Ruff – thick hair around neck.

Toy – very small breed.

Undercoat – soft, furry hair under outer hair of some breeds.

INTERNET LINKS

If you have access to the Internet, you can visit these websites to find out more about dogs. For links to these sites, go to the Usborne Quicklinks Website at **www.usborne-quicklinks.com** and enter the keywords "spotters dogs".

Internet safety

When using the Internet, please follow the **Internet safety guidelines** shown on the Usborne Quicklinks Website.

WEBSITE 1 Find out all about dogs, discover which dog is right for you, then test your knowledge.

WEBSITE 2 An interactive guide to looking after a dog.

WEBSITE 3 A slide show about puppies.

WEBSITE 4 Everything you need to know about buying and caring for a puppy, with video clips and animations.

WEBSITE 5 A quiz about working dogs.

WEBSITE 6 Training tips, video clips, stories and a question and answer page all about dogs.

WEBSITE 7 Watch video clips from Crufts, the international Championship dog show, then design your own dog breed.

WEBSITE 8 Meet a gang of virtual dogs, play dog games and download dog-care leaflets.

WEBSITE 9 Learn about the different breeds of dogs.

WEBSITE 10 Discover dog facts and explore the history of the dog family.

SPOTTER'S CHART

The dogs on this chart are arranged in alphabetical order. When you see one, write down the date you spotted it in the space next to the name.

Name of breed	Date	Name of breed	Date
Affenpinscher		Elkhound	
Alaskan Malamute		Foxhound	
Anatolian Karabash		German Shepherd Dog	
Basenji		Great Dane	
Basset Griffon Vendéen		Greyhound	
Beagle		Greyhound, Italian	
Bichon Frise		Griffon Brabançon	
Bloodhound		Griffon Bruxellois	
Borzoi		Groenendael	
Bouvier des Flandres		Hound, Afghan	
Boxer		Hound, Basset	
Briard		Hound, Ibizan	
Bulldog		Hound, Pharaoh	
Bulldog, French		Husky, Siberian	
Bullmastiff		Japanese Chin	
Cattle Dog, Australian		Keeshond	
Chihuahua, Long-coat		Kelpie	
Chihuahua, Smooth-coat		Komondor	
Chinese Crested Dog		Kuvasz	
Chow Chow		Leonberger	
Collie, Bearded		Lhasa Apso	
Collie, Border		Löwchen	
Collie, Rough		Lurcher	
Collie, Smooth		Malinois	
Corgi, Cardigan		Maltese	
Corgi, Pembroke		Maremma	
Dachshund, Long-haired		Mountain Dog, Bernese	
Dachshund, Smooth-haired		Mountain Dog, Estrela	
Dachshund, Wire-haired		Mountain Dog, Pyrenean	
Dalmatian		Münsterlander, Large	
Deerhound		Münsterlander, Small	
Dobermann		Newfoundland	
Drentse Patrijshond		Norwegian Buhund	

Name of breed	Date	Name of breed	Date
Otterhound		Spaniel, King Charles	
Papillon		Spaniel, Sussex	
Pekingese		Spaniel, Tibetan	
Pinscher, Miniature		Spaniel, Welsh Springer	
Pointer		Spitz, Finnish	
Pointer, German, Short-haired		Terrier, Airedale	
Pomeranian		Terrier, Australian	
Poodle, Miniature		Terrier, Australian Silky	
Poodle, Standard		Terrier, Bedlington	
Poodle, Toy		Terrier, Border	
Pug		Terrier, Boston	
Puli		Terrier, Bull	
Retriever, Chesapeake Bay		Terrier, Cairn	
Retriever, Curly-coated		Terrier, Dandie Dinmont	
Retriever, Flat-coated		Terrier, English Toy	
Retriever, Golden		Terrier, Fox, Smooth-coat	
Retriever, Labrador		Terrier, Fox, Wire-coat	
Rhodesian Ridgeback		Terrier, Irish	
Rottweiler		Terrier, Jack Russell	
St Bernard		Terrier, Kerry Blue	
Saluki		Terrier, Lakeland	
Samoyed		Terrier, Manchester	
Schipperke		Terrier, Norfolk	
Schnauzer, Giant		Terrier, Norwich	
Schnauzer, Miniature		Terrier, Scottish	
Schnauzer, Standard		Terrier, Sealyham	
Setter, English		Terrier, Staffordshire Bull	
Setter, Gordon		Terrier, Tibetan	
Setter, Irish		Terrier, Welsh	
Sheepdog, Old English		Terrier, West Highland	
Sheepdog, Shetland		Terrier, Yorkshire	
Shih Tzu		Tervueren	
Sloughi		Vallhund	
Spaniel, American Cocker		Vizsla	
Spaniel, Brittany		Weimeraner	
Spaniel, Cavalier King Charles		Whippet	
Spaniel, Clumber		Wolfhound, Irish	
Spaniel, Cocker			
Spaniel, English Springer			
Spaniel, Field			
Spaniel, Irish Water			

INDEX OF BREEDS